Hills, Holes, Honks and Beeps

RAY RAGGIANI

Copyright © 2020 Ray Raggiani
All rights reserved
First Edition

PAGE PUBLISHING, INC.
Conneaut Lake, PA

First originally published by Page Publishing 2020

ISBN 978-1-64462-044-1 (pbk)
ISBN 978-1-64462-045-8 (digital)

Printed in the United States of America

Dedicated to all the men, women, and children lost to preventable accidents on construction sites.

Hello, my name is Jack, and this is my family, dad, mom and my little sister, Emma. Oh yes! I can't forget our dog, Mr. Chili Pepper.

Today is the first day in our new home. Mom tells us to go play soccer outside. Dad reminds us to be careful and to put on safety shin guards for protection.

Do you wear safety protection? Emma and I wear shin guards when we play soccer. I have green ones, and Emma wears yellow ones. Emma kicks the soccer ball far over the net.

"Oh no, Jack, my ball went way down in that deep hole! What do I do?"

Jack says, "I'll go tell a grown-up!"

"Good job telling us about that hole," Mom said. "Now let's call the construction workers to help us."

Never climb into any kind of a hole or trench. They are very dangerous.

Shortly after, some workers arrived to help us. They were all dressed in shiny reflective vests, glasses, boots and hard hats. This safety gear is what workers wear to protect themselves from getting hurt. One of the workers told us not to worry because they would get our ball back safely.

Willy and Walter wiggle the ball. Kids, can you wiggle like a worm?

Wow, great job!

Hey, Chili is climbing a big hill.

That looks fun. Let's climb too.

Stop! Hills can be very dangerous, like holes. They can come crashing down on you! Keep off them! (*Boing! Bang! Bonk!*)

*Beep! Beep! Honk! Honk!
Rumble! Rumble!*
What is that noise?
Let's get out of here!

Oh no, Walter, here comes a big yellow monster.

That's no monster. It's a big backhoe digger. Hurry, run away!

I can't run! I have no legs.

The backhoe driver beeps and honks his horn making chili run home faster than a cheetah. Soon the backhoe begins to fill in the dangerous hole with lots of rocks and dirt.

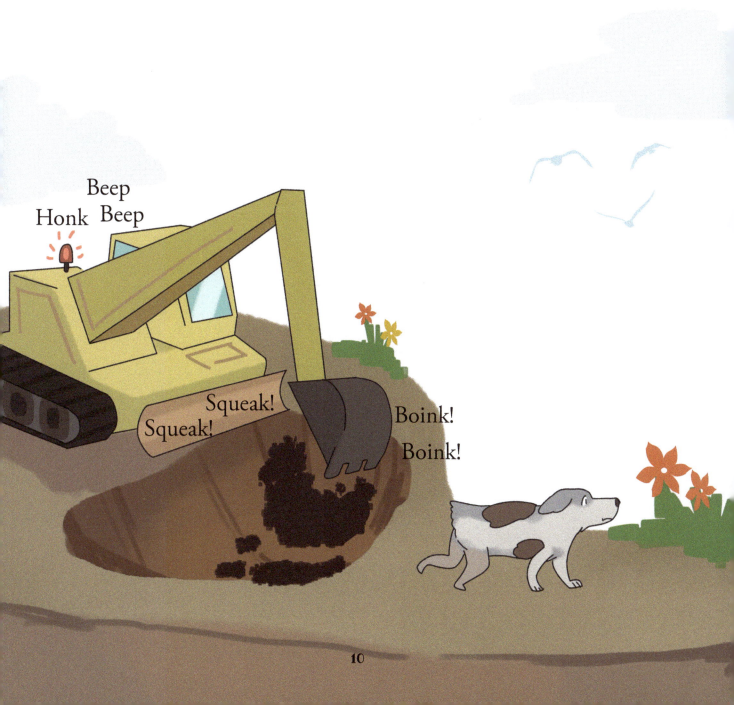

Just then, we heard another rumble. Everyone started to laugh. It was our tummies. Mom said we better get home for dinner. We thanked the workers and headed home.

Wow! What a thrilling first day in our new home. We learned that it's always important to wear our safety gear. We also learned never to play in any kinds of holes or trenches or climb on construction hills, because these places can be very unsafe and dangerous and always call a grown up for help. Our adventure today taught us that when we hear a beep or honk from trucks or tractors, we should move away to a safe area quickly and always remember never climb or hide in the digging buckets of any construction machines.

Your friends,
Jack, Emma, Willy, and Walter

We also learned worms do not have arms or legs.

1. Emergency _____
2. Fire department _____
3. Police department _____
4. Hospital _____
5. Doctor's office _____
6. Poison control _____
7. School number _____
8. Gas company _____
9. Electric company _____
10. Water department _____

About the Author

Raymond Raggiani lives in Berkley, Massachusetts, with his wife, three children, and dog, Chili. He has worked in the construction industry for over thirty-five years. His passion for safety leads him to write his first book, *Hills, Holes, Honks, and Beeps*. The goal of this story is to educate children and their families about the possible dangers of construction sites, with the hope of avoiding all preventable accidents.